Copyright © 1983 Beverley Parkin

Published by
Lion Publishing plc
Icknield Way, Tring, Herts, England
ISBN 0 85648 496 2
Lion Publishing Corporation
772 Airport Boulevard, Ann Arbor, Michigan 48106, USA
ISBN 0 85648 496 2
Albatross Books
PO Box 320, Sutherland, NSW 2232, Australia
ISBN 0 86760 310 0

First edition 1983
Reprinted 1983

Photographs by Lion Publishing/Jon Willcocks

Printed in Italy
by International Publishing Enterprises Rome

Say it
with Flowers

BEVERLEY PARKIN

A LION BOOK

Flowers—with love

Many years ago I lay on a hospital bed unable to move —
paralysed and facing the threat of being put into an iron
lung. Outside one of the worst November fogs clung to the
full-length windows. I think I wanted to die. My brain was very active
and the pictures it produced were depressing, to say the least!

Next day flowers started to arrive, until there were banks of them
around me. They could have seemed funereal but to me they spoke
of life and love. I could not see them very clearly, as my specs had
been removed, but their colour and fragrance helped to will me back
to hope and, eventually, a full healthy life with a minimal physical
handicap.

Flowers play a precious part in my personal memory 'box'.
Our wedding flowers, congratulatory sprays when the children were
born, hot sticky fingers clutching a bunch of daffodils on mothers'
day, sweetly perfumed freesias — or the first rose, plucked from our
garden and proudly presented by my husband. Then there were the
white roses I arranged as a special tribute for my father when he died,
placed with such love and gratitude for all that he was.

So many memories — happy and sad — not only for myself but
for others too, as I have been allowed to express their love to family
and friends, on birth, death, marriage, and illness. Flowers are a love
offering when they are given with a full heart.

*Dear Lord, may the gifts you have given us be used to express
your love for others.*

❝ Flowers appear on the earth;
the season of singing
has come, the cooing of doves is heard in our land. **❞**
FROM THE SONG OF SOLOMON

The joy of God's creation

It was my grandfather who introduced me to a love of flowers —
aided and abetted by my grandmother. She specially loved
pansies (violas). To her, every flower had an individual face.

She would pack sandwiches and grandfather and I would sally
forth into the gentle hills to see what we could find. Grandad would
say, 'You are nearer the ground than me, young'un; use your eyes.'

It was on these hills I first saw primroses, violets and cowslips
and, later in the year, bluebells, hazel catkins and many other delights.
As the year grew warmer we would lie among the poppies in the long
grass and listen to the larks singing overhead. We blew dandelion
'clocks' to tell the time and tried to think whose feet would fit into the
delicate cups of 'ladies slippers'. Soon we picked blackberries and
exclaimed over the autumn cobwebs which festooned the hedgerows,
glistening in the low sun.

Grandfather was a cabinet-maker who delighted in craftsman-
ship and the texture of wood. As he grew older his veined hands
would tenderly caress the patina of old age on a piece of furniture
and say, 'That's a nice bit of stuff, duck.'

Today the hills we explored are nearly covered by housing estates.
I do hope my little wild flowers are not just thrown away as weeds.

*Thank you, Lord, for those who teach us the joys of your
creation. Help us not to be too busy to see the little everyday
wonders that surround us.*

66 Consider how the lilies grow.
They do not labour or spin.
Yet I tell you, not even Solomon in all his splendour
was dressed like one of these. **99**

FROM LUKE'S GOSPEL, CHAPTER 12

Feeling the heartbeat

Have you noticed how many medical programmes there seem to be on television these days? Whether it's a documentary or a soap opera, out comes the stethoscope, the hand on the pulse and the blood-pressure meter. We are all fascinated to know whether the patient's heart is beating in the correct rhythm.

Before and after my babies were born their heartbeats were monitored. On returning home, if the baby was quieter than usual, I would tip-toe to the cot to make sure he was actually breathing.

A heart beating rhythmically is a very reassuring sound. Perhaps it stems from the time we were in our mother's womb, tucked up against her heart. We hold our babies to us; we demonstrate our love for others by hugging them; we comfort children and adults alike by holding them against us — and we all need this demonstrative affection.

The other day someone asked a rather surprising question. 'Do you know what it is like to be cuddled by God?' It is an experience that words alone cannot describe. But it fulfils the promises God has given us in the Bible when, in the midst of physical or emotional turmoil, there is God's 'heartbeat' and a sense of warmth and security surrounding us.

But he has given us free will. Whether we accept his love in Jesus and come to him is up to each one of us individually. Do *you* know what it is like to be 'cuddled by God'?

Dear Father, please keep us close to you whatever the circumstances. May each of us be as a child, held close to the heart of a loving Father.

66 One of his disciples, whom Jesus loved, was lying close to the breast of Jesus. 99

FROM JOHN'S GOSPEL, CHAPTER 13

The awkward ones

Recently I was discussing childhood with a friend and we found we had one particular experience in common. We each had a child who had decided to leave home before the age of five! Having packed their little bags they toddled through the door. One hid in an outside cupboard before he decided to return to the family. Another asked her mother to help her cross the road, decided it was not worth the effort and agreed she would wait until she was older! It's interesting that even in the most loving of homes rebellious independence rears its head. There is an urge to turn and run from authority.

When I am arranging flowers and I come across a stem which is a difficult shape I try to use it in a prominent position, to add interest and character to the display, but without dominating the whole. Children, rather like the awkward flower, need to be guided lovingly, gently but firmly, into their place within the family relationship. And we adults need directing, too, if we are to find God's place for us in his family and in the world.

Dear Lord, when life seems difficult and we are tempted to run away from reality, please watch over us. Use even our awkwardness and inadequacy as part of your plan for us.

66 Trust in the Lord with all your heart
and lean not on your
own understanding; in all your ways acknowledge him,
and he will make your paths straight.99

FROM PROVERBS, CHAPTER 3

Such lavish beauty

Every year I wait with excited anticipation for the flowering cherry trees to break into blossom. The sight of the pink-and-white flower-laden boughs against a blue sky brings a lump to my throat. The sheer perfection of beauty stops me in my tracks. As I lift my head to look at them the familiar phrase of 'drinking in' beauty just isn't enough. I want to lose myself in each perfect flower. As a child I used to scrape my knees climbing up into the branches. I would sit up there and read for hours in a perfect world of my own, populated with little green caterpillars, ants and early sleepy bees.

Now, alas, my tree-climbing days are over but I love to gather one or two branches of wild cherry when they are just in bud. After scraping and splitting the bottom of their stems I push them onto a pinholder to form a gentle curve — a feast for my eyes as the delicate white flowers shiver and tremble on their slender stems.

Thank you, Father, for such lavish beauty; for bluebell woods and springtime banks of daffodils. May our eyes never grow weary of looking, and our hearts of exulting, at the world you made.

66 You will go out in joy and be led forth in peace; the mountains and hills will burst into song before you, and all the trees of the field will clap their hands. **99**
FROM ISAIAH, CHAPTER 55

Household treasures

L ast winter our garden was covered with snow and the birds had a hard time. We put out nuts and other goodies for them, but the squirrels kept running off with the food.

Watching the squirrels reminded me of a time in Canada. Sitting on the balcony of a chalet in the pine-strewn Rocky Mountains I put down my mug of half-finished coffee. I turned round a moment later to see a red bushy tail poking out of the top and its owner drinking the remaining dregs! Every morning my squirrel returned for its elevenses, growing bolder at every visit until we left. I hope he finds a warm resting-place in the windswept snow-laden mountains this winter.

Our family are just like that red squirrel — storing and hoarding all sorts of articles that may 'come in useful'. The boys' bedrooms are full of odd nuts and bolts and unidentifiable pieces of metal and wood; and my daughter's room is a conglomerate of babyhood playthings, hair-ribbons, pretty bottles without lids, and chipped ornaments which cannot possibly be thrown away.

I am the worst hoarder of them all. No piece of interesting wood, shell, dried flower or material is ever disposed of. No wonder the cupboards are overflowing! Some day soon I must really have a clear out. After all, I'm meant to be storing up treasures in heaven, not all around the house.

Dear Lord, help us not to hoard possessions but to share them. Help us to remember where our real treasure is and to clear away the rubbish which so quickly clutters up our lives.

66 Where your treasure is, there your heart will be also. **99**

FROM LUKE'S GOSPEL, CHAPTER 12

A sure foundation

One of the disadvantages of demonstrating flower arranging in public, as I do, is that when you make mistakes everybody knows! The nightmare that most arrangers dread is having the foundation material collapse just as a display is completed! You step back to look at the full effect and a second later your beautiful orderly arrangement is nothing but a mass of sad-looking flowers and crumpled stems. I am thankful to say this has not happened often in my experience. I hope it never will again — but I have learned to say, 'Well, that's life!'

That *is* life , isn't it? Just when we least expect it, our little world falls apart. There is the unexpected phone call telling us that someone we love has died or is very ill. A friend or one of the family is made redundant. A policeman stands at the door saying, 'Don't be alarmed, Madam, but...'. Or, on a lesser scale, the car breaks down in the middle of a busy junction!

How do we react when things go wrong? Do we collapse into a state of shock? Or have we experienced enough of God's love and help in similar situations to have our spiritual and emotional foundations firmly rooted in him — not in people, places or things.

Dear Father, thank you that as we learn to love you, we find
you loving and faithful. Please forgive us when we worry or
are anxious and don't let you deal with the situation.
Thank you that you have everything under control.

66 Be my rock of refuge,
to which I can always go;
give the command to save me, for you are my rock
and my fortress. **99**
FROM PSALM 71

Touch of spring

One of the most beautiful sights in spring is the green blush that begins to appear on the hedgerows. Our senses quicken at the promise of warmer days to come. The dark buds of the alder, hornbeam and oak form a miraculous leaf within their tight mantle. The handsome sticky buds of the horse-chestnut are a real harbinger of spring as their outer casing gradually peels back to show a tiny fan of leaves ready to spring out into a graceful parasol of green. I often bring bare branches of forsythia and flowering currant indoors in the warmth to enjoy their flowers early.

Every time I am able to share the love of Jesus with others — I have a mental image of spring. I see each person as a bud ready to be warmed by God's love and 'watered' by his Holy Spirit. Layer upon layer of pre-conceived ideas, hurt feelings, loneliness, pain and rejection are gradually eased away until the human spirit opens up, yielding to the love of God, and blossoming under his hand.

Dear Father — even as our hearts lift in response to the spring and new life — please keep us soft and pliable towards you — ready to accept your direction.

66 Sing to the Lord with thanksgiving;
make music to our God on the harp. He covers the sky with clouds;
he supplies the earth with rain and makes grass grow on the hills. **99**
FROM PSALM 147

Time to reflect

Many years ago my brother built a cottage on a Scottish island. Remote and windswept, it is one of the most beautiful places on God's earth — when the sun shines! During the following summer holidays we found many wild flowers we had seen before only in books. And we had fun collecting shells, lichen and dry sea-bleached wood to make a collage to hang on the wall. It is still there now — a reminder of the time when the children were small and of stories round the big log fire.

As the years have gone by, we have had to give up the log fire for a more practical stove which heats by night and day. But the landscape and the flowers never change — and the sea still washes the shell-sand bay.

Occasionally there are storm-force winds that edge and drive the water between rocks and into crannies, creating deeper channels. Water swirls the seaweed fronds, scattering the myriad sea creatures that shelter there. Each rock pool is like a tiny world. Sea anemones, prawns and baby squid, hermit crabs, winkles, silver eels, all trying to evade the eye as eager fingers lift the seaweed around the edges. Herons perch on the rocks and seals play in the bay. Oyster-catchers and guillemots circle overhead.

On the island there is peace and tranquillity; time to read, paint, think and draw strength from the timelessness of the surrounding sea and land.

Lord — thank you for holidays, for giving us time to think and put life into perspective.

66 Mightier than the thunder of the great waters, mightier than the breakers of the sea — the Lord on high is mighty. **99**

FROM PSALM 93

Shelter

Near my home there is a large house with extensive grounds. When the estate was taken over by the present occupants, it was run-down and overgrown. Since then, year by year, the undergrowth has gradually been removed and the imaginative vision of the original gardener once again revealed. I love to visit the gardens to enjoy the beauty of early magnolia blossoms, lime flowers, wild daffodils, primroses and violets. I pay a yearly visit to the furthest part of the grounds to see one of the largest surviving cedars of Lebanon.

Its trunk has a tremendous girth, and as I sit at its base and gaze up into the branches, I have a great sense of permanence and strength. Stroking the bark I am aware of the hundreds of years of stored memories trapped in its tree rings. The tree pulsates with a life of its own, as well as the lives of the children who find perches amongst its lower limbs.

My own inner restlessness is soothed by the tree's maturity and majesty. Violets and windflowers lift their heads all around, and I find peace in the knowledge that my God is the creator of all things.

Lord, thank you for this tree — and all trees. May we see them as a token of your unfailing, steadfast love, in which we can shelter and find rest.

66 The righteous will flourish like a palm tree, they will grow like a cedar of Lebanon; planted in the house of the Lord, they will flourish in the courts of our God. **99**

FROM PSALM 92

Light and shade

Light and the ability to see are two of God's greatest gifts to us. But darkness too can be a blessing. When we cannot see, our other senses become sharper: we are more sensitive to sounds, tastes, smells and the things we touch. And of course with our eyes closed it is much easier to concentrate.

The feel of a rose petal is at once more delicate, its scent more beautiful. The curve of a cheek, the soft down on the back of a hand, a heart beating — all these assume a greater importance. We find a new experience in the notes of a dearly-loved piece of music or the first strawberry of the season.

As a child, though, I was terrified of going for a walk on dark evenings in case something unmentionable should drop on my head from the trees above me! The thought of a permanently dark world without sight and colour appals me — yet I sink gratefully into the darkness of sleep. Pain reduces me to a shivering wreck, yet without it I might never know the joy of being pain free.

Light and dark, love and hate, joy and pain, good and evil — these opposites balance one another.

We see this in the world of nature — though we don't always appreciate it. So next time I see a caterpillar chomping its way through my rose leaves, I am going to visualize the beautiful butterfly in the making!

Dear Lord, in difficult times, please help us to adapt. Give us new understanding. May we surrender ourselves utterly into your hands — that your loving purposes may be worked out.

66 We know that in all things
God works for the good of those who love him, who have been called
according to his purpose. **99**
FROM ROMANS, CHAPTER 8

Fishy business!

Years ago there was a fish shop in our village — open to the road — with a large marble slab, white and glistening. Bright red lobsters, crabs, prawns and pink shrimps were arranged with an artist's hand; white fish edged with parsley and lemons; winkles and cockles piled in heaps. During the shooting season pheasant and grouse would be strung up above the slab. The men in their straw hats and the lady in the little kiosk seemed immune to the all-pervading smell of fish.

Then one day the marble slab was no more to be seen. All that remained was the memory of the sea-harvest, a little door in the shutter, and a smell of fish. The village missed the colourful display and the pleasure of chatting in the queue.

The property came up 'For Sale'. The door was opened and we stepped inside, with agent's particulars in hand. The marble slab had gone, and the large china sinks. The back yard was covered in brambles and briars. All had been well scrubbed but still the smell of fish overwhelmed us!

Now a dream has become reality. Once again the shop is open and part of the community — now with a bow-fronted window full of pretty gifts and an open Bible. Our local folk and visitors enjoy coffee and home-made cakes while books, crafts, flowers and cards line the walls — a tempting array for sale. Some just come for a chat, some to buy. But we pray daily that the fragrance of Christ's love will spread out from it to the whole neighbourhood and community.

Dear Lord, may those of us who have known your touch upon our lives be generous in sharing that joy with others and not keep it selfishly to ourselves. Please bless us all as we love and serve one another in your name.

66 'Come, follow me,' Jesus said, 'and I will make you fishers of men.' At once they left their nets and followed him. **99**

FROM MATTHEW'S GOSPEL, CHAPTER 4

Against all odds

One of the joys of summer is eating out of doors. As the family has increased, the little terrace beneath our kitchen window has become far too small for the children and their friends — all now tall and strong with limitless appetites! For a long time we idly talked of building a proper area for seating, but nothing was done until one day when, in a spirit of enthusiasm, our sons took off their shirts, enrolled their friends — and girlfriends — and got digging. With Mum and Dad shouting encouragement from the sidelines and providing inexhaustible supplies of cold drinks and food, the allocated space was cleared.

Concrete slabs were painstakingly laid and all the helpers scratched their initials into the wet cement. A barbecue, capable of feeding all and sundry, was built into a wall. Soon after the completion of this new dining area, of course, the weather changed! We had to wait until the following year to enjoy the out-of-doors life again. But it has been a great success.

Much to my disgust, however, I soon noticed a tiny little plant worming its way through a minute crack in the cement. The ground was well prepared and the foundation was really thick, but this little seed had managed to germinate and find its way up to the light. The strength that takes defies imagination!

Jesus tells us in the Bible that the tiniest seed of faith can move mountains! Although our faith may waver, God promises help and strength to all who ask.

Father, may the tenacity of this little weed give us a fresh sense of your power and courage to trust you when circumstances threaten to overwhelm us.

66 Let us fix our eyes on Jesus, the author and perfector of our faith, who for the joy set before him endured the cross, scorning its shame, and sat down at the right hand of the throne of God. 99

FROM HEBREWS, CHAPTER 12

Water

ater is a very precious commodity. Those of us who live in a moderate climate tend to take rain for granted. But drier climates, feeling the touch of hunger, cry out for water and the fertility it brings.

There are few things more beautiful than a drop of water poised and trembling on the edge of a leaf, or raindrops running races down a pane of glass. I have watched thunderstorms over mountains and seas and experienced the exhilaration of sitting in the prow of a power-boat with the wind and spray whipping my hair and face. Yet all these things are mere glimpses of the power of God.

My husband loves water and fish. Whenever we pass a bridge over a stream we have to stop and peer over the edge. It may be a turgid canal or a fast-flowing river, with powerful currents pulling the weeds through the water like beautifully-combed hair. Occasionally we glimpse a fish and he is lost in delight as he watches it sporting around the stones.

We have a pond in the garden, lit by an outside lamp. After rain, on a still warm night, it is a magical place with satin-textured water. Moths flutter around the plants. The different shades of green leaves sparkle with diamond-drops of water, glistening and gleaming in the light. The goldfish congregate, lazily waving their fan-like tails. What a joy it is to revel in this little part of creation and know that it will be gloriously replenished by God's bountiful rain.

Thank you, Father, for rain that fills our lakes and rivers and feeds the earth. Please forgive us when we forget the needs of others. And may the living water of your Holy Spirit revive and fill each one of your children throughout the world.

66 Jesus said to the woman at the well
'Everyone who drinks this water will be thirsty again,
but whoever drinks the water I give him will never thirst.
Indeed, the water I give him will become in him a spring of water
welling up to eternal life.' **99**
FROM JOHN'S GOSPEL, CHAPTER 4

The crystal pendant

One of my treasured possessions is a crystal pendant. Its facets catch the light and turn it into pools of colour. It is a beautiful object and gives great pleasure.

Personalities, too, are multi-faceted, like my pendant. The older we get, the more we learn about ourselves and, hopefully, the more understanding we become of others. It took me a number of years to realize that not everyone thought the way I did and it came as quite a shock! Each person is a very precious individual to God and he has given us all our different traits of character. Social background, home, school, and other influences play their part, building up layer on layer until the real person is almost lost to sight. Removing those concealing layers can be a painful process. We need the light of God's love to see ourselves as we really are.

Jesus says he is the light.

My pendant reveals its true beauty only when the light shines on it. It is like that with all of us. As we allow the light of Jesus to flood into our lives he makes those lives beautiful. The pity is that we hold so many things back from him. Pride and self-will stand in the way. We find it difficult to let him deal with our darkest thoughts, our arrogance, insecurities, doubts, our lack of love and compassion. As I place my pendant around my neck it reminds me that so many parts of my life still do not reflect Jesus. Is your life like that, too?

Dear Father, there are so many imperfections in our lives and personalities; thank you for loving us just as we are. Thank you that you are changing us, helping us to reflect your own character.

66 Jesus said, 'I am the light of the world. Whoever follows me will never walk in darkness, but will have the light of life.' 99

FROM JOHN'S GOSPEL, CHAPTER 8

The pruner

On holiday in France, we came upon fields and fields of sunflowers, bright and gleaming in the sunlight. They filled the air with an indefinable perfume, and the busy humming of bees. Some of the 'younger' flowers held their heads up proudly, soaking in the sun. The 'older' ones, grown heavy and ripe with age, bowed down, their faces filling with the seeds that would be crushed and broken into oil. Like people crowded together on the terraces at a football match, they swayed and turned to catch the last of the sunlight.

Vines, too, hugged the hillsides, some well pruned, gnarled and twisted, bearing the promise of a good grape harvest. Young vines tenderly trained along wires, touched hands with their neighbours. Occasionally we came across vineyards choked with weeds, the branches growing long and straggly, with only minute clusters of grapes. The plants looked sad and neglected.

These fields reminded me so much of my own spiritual life I always want to be independent, to do 'my own thing'. I really need the discipline of God's word and his Spirit to make me useful to him. Difficulties and set-backs serve as pruning shears, cutting away all my 'wants' but providing for my needs. The fruits that are promised are love, joy, peace, patience, kindness, goodness, faithfulness, gentleness, and self-control — well worth the pain of pruning. God asks only that we allow him to work within us. What a relief that we do not have to strive and strain for perfection but, like the sunflowers, simply lift our faces to the Sun.

Father, we are willing for all that you want to do in our lives. But please help us during the pruning times to trust that you know best and that you do all in perfect love.

66 Jesus said, ' I am the vine; you are the branches. If a man remains in me and I in him, he will bear much fruit; apart from me you can do nothing.' 99

FROM JOHN'S GOSPEL, CHAPTER 15

The potted palm

I'm glad that house plants are so popular. The differences in colour, leaf form and texture are a delight, and although it may seem hard work to water and feed them they pay dividends in return. For people who are housebound they provide a constant interest. They bring beauty and refreshment to offices, hospitals and public places. Hotel reception halls all around the world have islands where plants flourish. Large indoor shopping areas now employ landscape gardeners to make them more intimate and relaxing. It's good to look up and enjoy the symmetry of a palm tree as we stagger under the weight of the shopping baskets!

In certain parts of Europe silk plants are finding tremendous popularity. I have seen flowering almonds, willows and other trees reproduced so faithfully that I've had to touch them before I could believe they weren't real. But it can be very confusing. One lady had a silk cyclamen by her bed in hospital — and someone watered it every day!

If you have a dark corner where natural plants refuse to flourish, a mixture of real and artificial plants combined with a few fresh flowers can create an interesting focal point. Choose a container which is large and heavy enough to support all the wire stems and roots, leaving space to sink a container into the soil which will hold a water-filled pot for the fresh flowers.

Father, thank you for those to whom you have given 'green fingers', for the artistic and practical gifts which create beauty in public places and in our homes. Give us real appreciation and, in the midst of a busy day, may we find time to say thank you.

66 As the soil makes the sprout come up
and a garden causes seeds to grow, so the Sovereign Lord
will make righteousness and praise spring up
before all nations. **99**

FROM ISAIAH, CHAPTER 61

In all circumstances

Because I am slightly handicapped myself, I am often asked to visit others who are physically handicapped. It's difficult for the able-bodied to understand the sheer frustration of coping with even the simple functions in life. To begin with, everything takes longer and the concentration required is very tiring. Washing, dressing, bathing a baby, preparing and cooking a meal, housework, driving a car — even striking a box of matches — can be exhausting.

Concentration and patience are the key and these qualities are not acquired overnight! It is essential for all of us to think creatively and positively, but particularly if we are physically handicapped. We need to have a sense of achievement every day, especially at the beginning. It is an encouragement to go on to bigger things. Being anxious wastes valuable energy. We need to take one day at a time, constantly reminding ourselves that God loves us and knows exactly what is happening. We can trust him for the future and in the days that need to be lived through now.

Dear Father, the Bible tells us to give thanks in all circumstances. Sometimes this is very difficult. But we do want to praise you that you can lift our spirits above physical circumstances to rejoice in you. The presence of Jesus brings healing to our spirits and casts out bitterness and frustration. Thank you Father for your provision in our darkest days.

66 Do you not know? Have you not heard?
The Lord is the everlasting God, the Creator of the ends of the earth. He will not grow tired or weary, and his understanding no-one can fathom. He gives strength to the weary and increases the power of the weak. Even youths grow tired and weary, and young men stumble and fall; but those who hope in the Lord will renew their strength. They will soar on wings like eagles; they will run and not grow weary, they will walk and not be faint. 99

FROM ISAIAH, CHAPTER 40

Beyond Pain

Dutch elm disease has struck many lovely old elms in the country round us. Because of the damage that this little beetle has caused, young saplings and mature trees stand stark and leafless against the summer sky, waiting only for the wind and an axe to bring them down. The bark of the dead tree falls away exposing the work of the beetle, a delicate tracery of grooves almost beautiful in its deadly perfection, tunnelling toward the tender heart of the tree. The beetle grubs are intent on survival, caring nothing for their unwilling host.

In a line of dead trees one may escape the disease. There seems no particular reason, any more than there seems to be a reason why this person or that one — child or adult — has to suffer an incurable disease. One hears the cry, 'Why, why?' from a grief-stricken heart. To see a tiny child dying a painful death, or a beloved partner suffering or taken from us stretches our faith to the limit. Even Jesus cried out on the cross, 'Father, Father, why have you forsaken me?'

Pain, bitterness, desperate loneliness can invade and overwhelm us, making it difficult if not impossible to pray. Though time blunts the edge of unhappy memories, we are never the same people again.

None of us can hope entirely to escape life's tragedies. But the seedlings of the elm remind me that there is life after death, that we are in God's hands. I think that if I did not know and believe this truth, I would be afraid to love and care for anyone. But the promises of God extend to all. 'Come to me,' says Jesus, 'and I will give you rest.'

Dear Lord, in times of pain may we turn to you in faith, believing that you will never let us go. Please hear our silent plea for help.

66 For everyone born of God has overcome the world. This is the victory that has overcome the world, even our faith. Who is it that overcomes the world? Only he who believes that Jesus is the Son of God. 99

FROM THE FIRST LETTER OF JOHN, CHAPTER 5

Three flowers

One of my favourite flower arrangements uses just three flowers. It is not only economical, but shows each flower to perfection. Using a favourite piece of driftwood as backing, I choose my flowers with the smallest bloom at the top, then the second smallest, leading to the largest bloom at the base. A pinholder in a small dish holds each stem securely to the base.

This form of arrangement is quite different from the typical Western form of massed flowers. It owes its beginnings to the Japanese school of flower arrangement, which has a very long — and religious — history. The Japanese say we should never arrange flowers when we feel depressed and tense, as this communicates itself to others. When I handle flowers, however, I often find my anxieties are gradually soothed away — at least for the time being.

I use my three-flower display to spell out a three-word message: 'GOD LOVES YOU'. The great Creator God is a tender, loving Father. In his infinite love and grace he sent Jesus, his only Son, to give his life for us — to provide a way out of hopelessness, to make us at one with God. As I put the third and last flower in place it becomes you — me — loved by God, and given a whole new life in which to love him in return.

I often arrange these flowers against a background of thorns, to remind myself of the cost of God's love. He does not force us into submission. He wants us to be willing to trust in Jesus and through him find the path to heaven.

Father, thank you that in your love you sent Jesus, your Son, to save us from all we deserve. Thank you for the glorious fact of his resurrection. Thank you for the presence of Jesus in our lives. Please help us to give ourselves to you more and more.

66 I tell you the truth,
whoever hears my word and believes him who sent me, has eternal life
and will not be condemned; he has crossed over from death to life. **99**

FROM JOHN'S GOSPEL, CHAPTER 5